CW00726526

POCKET

PSALMS

GOD BLESS

POCKET

PSALMS

GOD BLESS

paternoster
publishing

HUNT&
THORPE

PART I

GOD IN THE PSALMS

GOD AND HIS CREATION

O Lord our Lord,
how excellent is thy name in all the earth!
who hast set thy glory above the heavens.

Out of the mouth of babes
and sucklings has thou ordained strength
because of thine enemies, that thou mightest still
the enemy and the avenger.

When I consider thy heavens,
the work of thy fingers, the moon and the stars,
which thou hast ordained;

What is man, that thou art mindful of him?
and the son of man, that thou visitest him?
For thou hast made him a little lower
than the angels, and hast crowned him
with glory and honour.

•

O Lord our Lord,
how excellent is thy name in all the earth!

FROM PSALM 8

GOD AND HIS SUFFERING

⊷⊶◉⊷⊶

$\mathcal{M}$y God, my God,
why hast thou forsaken me?
why art thou so far from helping me,
and from the words of my roaring?
O my God, I cry in the daytime,
but thou hearest not;
and in the night season,
and am not silent.

⊶◉⊶

All they that see me laugh me to scorn:
they shoot out the lip,
they shake the head, saying,
He trusted on the Lord
that he would deliver him:

let him deliver him,
seeing he delighted in him.
They part my garments among them,
and cast lots upon my vesture.

. ◆ .

Ye that fear the Lord, praise him;
all ye the seed of Jacob,
glorify him; and fear him,
all ye the seed of Israel.
For he hath not despised nor
abhorred the affliction of the afflicted;
neither hath he hid his face from him;
but when he cried unto him, he heard.

FROM PSALM 22

GOD AND HIS FORGIVENESS

–•–◎◎◎◎–•–

*B*lessed is he whose transgression
is forgiven, whose sin is covered.
Blessed is the man unto whom
the Lord imputeth not iniquity,
and in whose spirit there is no guile.

–•◎•–

When I kept silence, my bones waxed
old through my roaring all the day long.
For day and night thy hand
was heavy upon me: my moisture
is turned into the drought of summer.

–•◎•–

I acknowledged my sin unto thee,
and mine iniquity have I not hid.
I said, I will confess my transgressions
unto the Lord; and thou forgavest
the iniquity of my sin.

⋅✦⋅

Be glad in the Lord,
and rejoice, ye righteous:
and shout for joy,
all ye that are upright in heart.

FROM PSALM 32

GOD AND HIS GOODNESS

❧⟴⟴❧

I will bless the Lord at all times:
his praise shall continually be in my mouth.
My soul shall make her boast in the Lord:
the humble shall hear thereof, and be glad.

⟴

O magnify the Lord with me,
and let us exalt his name together.
I sought the Lord, and he heard me,
and delivered me from all my fears.
They looked unto him, and were lightened:
and their faces were not ashamed.
This poor man cried, and the Lord heard him,
and saved him out of all his troubles.

⟴

The angel of the Lord encampeth round about
them that fear him, and delivereth them.
O taste and see that the Lord is good:
blessed is the man that trusteth in him.

· ❖ ·

O fear the Lord, ye his saints:
for there is no want to them that fear him.
The young lions do lack, and suffer hunger:
but they that seek the Lord
shall not want any good thing.

FROM PSALM 34

GOD AND HIS GLORY

❧⟶⊙⟵❧

$\mathcal{G}$reat is the Lord, and greatly
to be praised in the city of our God,
in the mountain of his holiness.
God is known in her palaces for a refuge.

•❖•

According to thy name, O God,
so is thy praise unto the ends of the earth:
thy right hand is full of righteousness.
Let mount Zion rejoice,
let the daughters of Judah be glad,
because of thy judgments.

•❖•

Walk about Zion,
and go round about her:
tell the towers thereof.
Mark ye well her bulwarks,
consider her palaces;
that ye may tell it to
the generation following.

❖

For this God is our God
for ever and ever:
he will be our guide
even unto death.

FROM PSALM 48

GOD AND HIS WORD

◆━◆━◆

*W*herewithal shall a young man
cleanse his way? by taking heed
thereto according to thy word.
With my whole heart have I sought thee:
O let me not wander
from thy commandments.

◆━◆

Thy word have I hid in mine heart,
that I might not sin against thee.
Blessed art thou, O Lord:
teach me thy statutes.

◆━◆

With my lips have I declared
all the judgments of thy mouth.
I have rejoiced in the
way of thy testimonies,
as much as in all riches.

· ❦ ·

I will meditate in thy precepts,
and have respect unto thy ways.
I will delight myself in thy statutes:
I will not forget thy word.

FROM PSALM 119

GOD AND HIS LOVE

✦⟫═✺═⟪✦

O give thanks unto the Lord;
for he is good:
for his mercy endureth for ever.
O give thanks unto the God of gods:
for his mercy endureth for ever.
O give thanks to the Lord of lords:
for his mercy endureth for ever.

✦

To him who alone doeth great wonders:
for his mercy endureth for ever.
To him that by wisdom made the heavens:
for his mercy endureth for ever.
To him that stretched out the earth above
the waters: for his mercy endureth for ever.

Who remembered us in our low estate:
for his mercy endureth for ever . . ..
Who giveth food to all flesh:
for his mercy endureth for ever.
O give thanks unto the God of heaven:
for his mercy endureth for ever.

FROM PSALM 136

GOD AND HIS GREATNESS

⊹⊱⋆⊰⊹

*G*reat is the Lord,
and greatly to be praised;
and his greatness is unsearchable.
One generation shall praise thy works
to another, and shall declare
thy mighty acts.

⋆⊹⋆

I will speak of the glorious honour
of thy majesty, and of thy wondrous works.
And men shall speak of the might
of thy terrible acts:
and I will declare thy greatness.

They shall abundantly utter
the memory of thy great goodness,
and shall sing of thy righteousness.

· ❖ ·

The Lord is gracious,
and full of compassion;
slow to anger,
and of great mercy.
The Lord is good to all:
and his tender mercies
are over all his works.

FROM PSALM 145

GOD AND HIS STRENGTH

⊸⊱⟨◉⟩⊰⊶

*T*ruly my soul waiteth upon God:
from him cometh my salvation.
He only is my rock and my salvation;
he is my defence;
I shall not be greatly moved.

·⊷·

My soul, wait thou only upon God;
for my expectation is from him.
He only is my rock and my salvation:
he is my defence;
I shall not be moved.
In God is my salvation and my glory:
the rock of my strength,
and my refuge, is in God.

Trust in him at all times; ye people,
pour out your heart before him:
God is a refuge for us.

· ❖ ·

God hath spoken once;
twice have I heard this;
that power belongeth unto God.
Also unto thee, O Lord, belongeth mercy:
for thou renderest to every man
according to his work.

FROM PSALM 62

GOD THE MESSIAH

❦

The Lord said unto my Lord,
Sit thou at my right hand,
until I make thine enemies thy footstool.
The Lord shall send the rod
of thy strength out of Zion:
rule thou in the midst of thine enemies.

❖

Thy people shall be willing
in the day of thy power,
in the beauties of holiness
from the womb of the morning:
thou hast the dew of thy youth.

The Lord hath sworn,
and will not repent,
Thou art a priest for ever after
the order of Melchizedek.

·❖·

He shall drink of the brook in the way:
therefore shall he lift up the head.

FROM PSALM 110

GOD AND HIS POWER

‹›—›◦‹—‹›

*H*e that dwelleth in the secret place
of the most High shall abide under
the shadow of the Almighty.
I will say of the Lord,
He is my refuge and my fortress:
my God; in him will I trust.

›»◦ FROM PSALM 91 ◦«‹

PART II
MY NEEDS AND THE PSALMS

WHEN I NEED GOD'S CARE

⊱⊰⊱⊰⊱⊰⊱⊰

$\mathcal{T}$he Lord is my shepherd;
I shall not want.
He maketh me to lie down in green pastures:
he leadeth me beside the still waters.

⊱⊰

He restoreth my soul: he leadeth me
in the paths of righteousness
for his name's sake.

⊱⊰

Yea, though I walk through the valley
of the shadow of death,
I will fear no evil: for thou art with me;
thy rod and thy staff they comfort me.

⊱⊰

Thou preparest a table before me
in the presence of mine enemies:
thou anointest my head with oil;
my cup runneth over.
Surely goodness and mercy
shall follow me all the days of my life:
and I will dwell in the
house of the Lord for ever.

PSALM 23

WHEN I NEED
GOD'S GUIDANCE

❖➤❍◗❒◖❖

*D*elight thyself also in the Lord;
and he shall give thee
the desires of thine heart.
Commit thy way unto the Lord;
trust also in him;
and he shall bring it to pass.

•❖•

And he shall bring forth
thy righteousness as the light,
and thy judgment as the noonday.
Rest in the Lord,
and wait patiently for him.

•❖•

The steps of a good man
are ordered by the Lord:
and he delighteth in his way.
Though he fall, he shall not
be utterly cast down:
for the Lord upholdeth
him with his hand.

FROM PSALM 37

WHEN I AM IN A PIT

꙳❯══◉══◉══❮꙳

I waited patiently for the Lord;
and he inclined unto me,
and heard my cry.
He brought me up
also out of an horrible pit,
out of the miry clay,
and set my feet upon a rock,
and established my goings.

•❉•

And he hath put a new song
in my mouth,
even praise unto our God:
many shall see it, and fear,
and shall trust in the Lord.

Many, O Lord my God,
are thy wonderful works
which thou hast done,
and thy thoughts which are to us-ward:
they cannot be reckoned up
in order unto thee:
if I would declare and speak of them,
they are more than can be numbered.

FROM PSALM 40

WHEN I WANT
TO PRAISE GOD

O sing unto the Lord a new song;
for he hath done marvellous things:
his right hand, and his holy arm,
hath gotten him the victory.
The Lord hath made known his salvation:
his righteousness hath he openly shewed
in the sight of the heathen.

He hath remembered his mercy
and his truth toward the house of Israel:
all the ends of the earth have seen
the salvation of our God.
Make a joyful noise unto the Lord,
all the earth: make a loud noise,
and rejoice, and sing praise.

⋅◦⋅

Sing unto the Lord with the harp;
with the harp, and the voice of a psalm.
With trumpets and sound of cornet
make a joyful noise before
the Lord, the King.

FROM PSALM 98

WHEN I AM DEPRESSED

~·>≡◎≡<·~

*A*s the hart panteth
after the water brooks,
so panteth my soul after thee, O God.
My soul thirsteth for God,
for the living God: when shall I come
and appear before God?

·◈·

My tears have been
my meat day and night,
while they continually say unto me,
Where is thy God?

·◈·

When I remember these things,
I pour out my soul in me:
for I had gone with the multitude,
I went with them to the house of God,
with the voice of joy and praise,
with a multitude that kept holyday.

·•·

Why art thou cast down, O my soul?
and why art thou disquieted in me?
hope thou in God:
for I shall yet praise him
for the help of his countenance.

FROM PSALM 42

WHEN I HAVE SINNED

❧━━◉━━❧

*H*ave mercy upon me, O God,
according to thy lovingkindness:
according unto the multitude of thy
tender mercies blot out my transgressions.
Wash me throughly from mine iniquity,
and cleanse me from my sin.

•━•

For I acknowledge my transgressions:
and my sin is ever before me.
Against thee, thee only, have I sinned,
and done this evil in thy sight . . ..

•━•

Hide thy face from my sins,
and blot out all mine iniquities.
Create in me a clean heart, O God;
and renew a right spirit within me.

Cast me not away from thy presence;
and take not thy holy spirit from me.
Restore unto me the joy of thy salvation;
and uphold me with thy free spirit.

FROM PSALM 51

WHEN I AM UPSET

❖

They compassed me about
also with words of hatred; and
fought against me without a cause.

⋅❖⋅

But do thou for me, O God the Lord,
for thy name's sake:
because thy mercy is good,
deliver thou me.
For I am poor and needy,
and my heart is wounded within me.

⋅❖⋅

I am gone like the shadow
when it declineth:
I am tossed up and down as the locust.
My knees are weak through fasting;
and my flesh faileth of fatness.
I became also a reproach unto them:
when they looked upon me
they shaked their heads.

⋅❖⋅

Help me, O Lord my God:
O save me according to thy mercy:
That they may know that this is thy hand;
that thou, Lord, hast done it.

FROM PSALM 109

WHEN I AM LONELY

Unto thee, O Lord, do I lift up my soul.
O my God, I trust in thee:
let me not be ashamed, let not mine enemies
triumph over me.

The meek will he guide in judgment:
and the meek will he teach his way.
All the paths of the Lord are mercy
and truth unto such as keep his
covenant and his testimonies.

Mine eyes are ever toward the Lord;
for he shall pluck my feet out of the net.
Turn thee unto me, and have mercy upon me;
for I am desolate and afflicted.
The troubles of my heart are enlarged:
O bring thou me out of my distresses.
Look upon mine affliction and my pain;
and forgive all my sins.

•◦•

O keep my soul, and deliver me:
let me not be ashamed;
for I put my trust in thee.

FROM PSALM 25

WHEN I AM SAD

O Lord, rebuke me not in thine anger,
neither chasten me in thy hot displeasure.
Have mercy on me, O Lord; for I am weak:
O Lord, heal me; for my bones are vexed.

My soul is also sore vexed:
but thou, O Lord, how long?
Return, O Lord, deliver my soul:
oh save me for thy mercies' sake.

I am weary with my groaning;
all the night make I my bed to swim;
I water my couch with my tears.
Mine eye is consumed because of grief;
it waxeth old because of all mine enemies.

··•··

Depart from me, all ye workers of iniquity;
for the Lord hath heard
the voice of my weeping.
The Lord hath heard my supplication;
the Lord will receive my prayer.

FROM PSALM 6

WHEN I AM
BROKEN-HEARTED

⊷∺⊙⊜⊶

*P*raise ye the Lord: for it is good
to sing praises unto our God;
for it is pleasant; and praise is comely.
He healeth the broken in heart,
and bindeth up their wounds.

∙◦∙

He telleth the number of the stars;
he calleth them all by their names.
Great is our Lord, and of great power:
his understanding is infinite.
The Lord lifteth up the meek:
he casteth the wicked down to the ground.

∙◦∙

He delighteth not
in the strength of the horse:
he taketh not pleasure in
the legs of a man.
The Lord taketh pleasure
in them that fear him,
in those that hope in his mercy.
Praise the Lord, O Jerusalem;
praise thy God, O Zion.

He maketh peace in thy borders,
and filleth thee with the finest of the wheat.

FROM PSALM 147

WHEN I AM SEEKING GOD

❖—❦—❖

O God, thou art my God;
early will I seek thee:
my soul thirsteth for thee,
my flesh longeth for thee
in a dry and thirsty land,
where no water is;
To see thy power and thy glory,
so as I have seen thee in the sanctuary.

❖

Because thy lovingkindness
is better than life,
my lips shall praise thee.
Thus will I bless thee while I live:
I will lift up my hands in thy name.

My soul shall be satisfied
as with marrow and fatness;
and my mouth shall praise thee
with joyful lips:
When I remember thee upon my bed, and
meditate on thee
in the night watches.

·—·—·

Because thou hast been my help,
therefore in the shadow of thy wings
will I rejoice.
My soul followeth hard after thee:
thy right hand upholdeth me.

FROM PSALM 63

WHEN I NEED GOD'S HELP

❧⊷❦⊶❧

*I*n my distress I cried unto the Lord,
and he heard me.
Deliver my soul, O Lord,
from lying lips,
and from a deceitful tongue.

⊷❧⊶

What shall be given unto thee?
or what shall be done unto thee,
thou false tongue?
Sharp arrows of the mighty,
with coals of juniper.

⊷❧⊶

Woe is me, that I sojourn in Mesech,
that I dwell in the tents of Kedar!
My soul hath long dwelt with him
that hateth peace.
I am for peace: but when I speak,
they are for war.

FROM PSALM 120

WHEN I NEED PARDON

*Out of the depths
have I cried unto thee, O Lord.
Lord, hear my voice:
let thine ears be attentive
to the voice of my supplications.

If thou, Lord,
shouldest mark iniquities,
O Lord, who shall stand?
But there is forgiveness with thee,
that thou mayest be feared.

I wait for the Lord,
my soul doth wait,
and in his word do I hope.
My soul waiteth for the Lord
more than they that watch for
the morning:
I say, more than they
that watch for the morning.

•◦•

Let Israel hope in the Lord:
for with the Lord there is mercy,
and with him is plenteous redemption.
And he shall redeem Israel
from all his iniquities.

PSALM 130

WHEN I AM
BUILDING A HOME

❦

*E*xcept the Lord build the house,
they labour in vain that build it:
except the Lord keep the city,
the watchman waketh but in vain.

⚬

It is vain for you to rise up early,
to sit up late, to eat the bread of sorrows:
for so he giveth his beloved sleep.

⚬

Lo, children are an heritage of the Lord:
and the fruit of the womb is his reward.

FROM PSALM 127

PART III

MEDITATING ON THE PSALMS

CREATOR GOD

❧❦❧

*T*he heavens declare the glory of God;
and the firmament sheweth his handywork.
Day unto day uttereth speech,
and night unto night sheweth knowledge.

⚬❖⚬

There is no speech nor language,
where their voice is not heard.
Their line is gone out through all the earth,
and their words to the end of the world.

⚬❖⚬

In them hath he set a tabernacle for the sun,
which is as a bridegroom
coming out of his chamber, and rejoiceth
as a strong man to run a race.
His going forth is from
the end of the heaven,
and his circuit unto the ends of it:
and there is nothing hid
from the heat thereof.

FROM PSALM 19

OUR SAVIOUR

-⸱=⊕=⸱-

The Lord is my light and my salvation;
whom shall I fear?
the Lord is the strength of my life;
of whom shall I be afraid?
When the wicked, even mine enemies
and my foes, came upon me
to eat up my flesh, they stumbled and fell.

-⸱•⸱-

Though an host should encamp against me,
my heart shall not fear:
though war should rise against me,
in this will I be confident.
One thing have I desired of the Lord,
that will I seek after;

that I may dwell in the house of the Lord
all the days of my life,
to behold the beauty of the Lord,
and to inquire in his temple.

·◈·

When thou saidst, Seek ye my face;
my heart said unto thee,
Thy face, Lord, will I seek.
I had fainted, unless I had believed
to see the goodness of the Lord
in the land of the living.
Wait on the Lord: be of good courage,
and he shall strengthen thine heart:
wait, I say, on the Lord

◈◈ FROM PSALM 27 ◈◈

GOD'S WORD

*Wherewithal shall a young man
cleanse his way? by taking heed
thereto according to thy word.
With my whole heart have I sought thee:
O let me not wander
from thy commandments.

Thy word have I hid in mine heart,
that I might not sin against thee.
Blessed art thou, O Lord:
teach me thy statutes.

With my lips have I declared
all the judgments of thy mouth.
I have rejoiced in the way
of thy testimonies,
as much as in all riches.

·◆·

I will meditate in thy precepts,
and have respect unto thy ways.
I will delight myself in thy statues:
I will not forget thy word.

FROM PSALM 119

HISTORY

⟶⟫⟐⟐⟫⟐⟵

O give thanks unto the Lord;
call upon his name:
make known his deeds among the people.
Sing unto him,
sing psalms unto him:
talk ye of all his wondrous works.

⋯✦⋯

Glory ye in his holy name:
let the heart of them rejoice that seek the Lord.
Seek the Lord, and his strength:
seek his face evermore.

⋯✦⋯

Remember his marvellous works
that he hath done;
his wonders, and the judgments of his mouth;
O ye seed of Abraham his servant,
ye children of Jacob his chosen.

FROM PSALM 105

RIGHTEOUSNESS

Blessed is the man that walketh
not in the counsel of the ungodly,
nor standeth in the way of sinners,
nor sitteth in the seat of the scornful.
But his delight is in the law of the Lord;
and in his law doth
he meditate day and night.

And he shall be like a tree
planted by the rivers of water,
that bringeth forth his fruit in his season;
his leaf also shall not wither;
and whatsoever he doeth shall prosper.
For the Lord knoweth
the way of the righteous:
but the way of the ungodly
shall perish.

FROM PSALM 1

REMEMBERING OUR LORD

❖

I cried unto God with my voice,
even unto God with my voice;
and he gave ear unto me.
In the day of my trouble I sought the Lord:
my sore ran in the night, and ceased not:
my soul refused to be comforted.

•❖•

I remembered God,
and was troubled: I complained,
and my spirit was overwhelmed.

•❖•

And I said, This is my infirmity:
but I will remember the years
of the right hand of the most High.
I will remember the works of the Lord:
surely I will remember thy wonders of old.
I will meditate also of all thy work,
and talk of thy doings.

⋅◆⋅

Thou leddest thy people
like a flock by the hand
of Moses and Aaron.

FROM PSALM 77

BEING PARDONED

✦

Bless the Lord,
O my soul: and all that is within me,
bless his holy name.
Bless the Lord, O my soul,
and forget not all his benefits:

✦

Who forgiveth all thine iniquities;
who healeth all thy diseases;
Who redeemeth thy life from destruction;
who crowneth thee with
lovingkindness and tender mercies;
Who satisfieth thy mouth
with good things; so that thy youth
is renewed like the eagle's.

For as the heaven
is high above the earth,
so great is his mercy
toward them that fear him.
As far as the east is from the west,
so far hath he removed
our transgressions from us.

·•·

Like as a father pitieth his children,
so the Lord pitieth them that fear him.
For he knoweth our frame;
he remembereth that we are dust.

FROM PSALM 103

GOD'S WAY

✦⇥⊙⇤✦

*B*ow down thine ear,
O Lord, hear me:
for I am poor and needy.
Preserve my soul; for I am holy:
O thou my God, save thy servant
that trusteth in thee.

•✦•

Be merciful unto me, O Lord:
for I cry unto thee daily.
Rejoice the soul of thy servant:
for unto thee, O Lord,
do I lift up my soul.

•✦•

Teach me thy way, O Lord;
I will walk in thy truth:
unite my heart to fear thy name.
I will praise thee, O Lord my God,
with all my heart: and I will glorify
thy name for evermore.
For great is thy mercy toward me:
and thou hast delivered my soul
from the lowest hell.

 FROM PSALM 86

WORDS OF CONSOLATION

⟿⊙⊜⟿

*T*he Lord shall preserve thee
from all evil:
he shall preserve thy soul.
The Lord shall preserve thy going out
and thy coming in from this time forth,
and even for evermore.

•❖•

They that sow in tears shall reap in joy.

•❖•

The Lord upholdeth all that fall,
and raiseth up all those
that be bowed down.

•❖•

The Lord preserveth the strangers;
he relieveth the fatherless and widow . . ..

·•·

He healeth the broken in heart,
and bindeth up their wounds.
The Lord lifteth up the meek.

·•·

FROM PSALMS 121; 126; 145; 146; 147

PROMISES

✦

*T*he law of the Lord is perfect,
converting the soul: the testimony
of the Lord is sure,
making wise the simple.

•✦•

For in the time of trouble
he shall hide me in his pavilion:
in the secret of his tabernacle
shall he hide me;
he shall set me up upon a rock.

•✦•

I will instruct thee and teach thee
in the way which thou shalt go:
I will guide thee with mine eye.

Be ye not as the horse, or as the mule,

which have no understanding:

whose mouth must be held

in with bit and bridle,

lest they come near unto thee.

⋅◦⋅

Behold, the eye of the Lord

is upon them that fear him,

upon them that hope in his mercy.

⋅◦⋅

The Lord is nigh unto all them

that call upon him,

to all that call upon him in truth.

FROM PSALMS 19; 27; 32; 33;145

JESUS

❖✦❖

*M*y God, my God,
why hast thou forsaken me?
why art thou so far from helping me,
and from the words of my roaring?

✦❖✦

All they that see me laugh me to scorn:
they shoot out the lip,
they shake the head, saying,
He trusted on the Lord
that he would deliver him:
let him deliver him,
seeing he delighted in him.

✦❖✦

They part my garments among them,
and cast lots upon my vesture.

⁘

The Lord said unto my Lord,
Sit thou at my right hand,
until I make thine enemies thy footstool.
The Lord hath sworn, and will not repent,
Thou art a priest for ever after
the order of Melchizedek.
Blessed be he that cometh
in the name of the Lord;
we have blessed you
out of the house of the Lord.

FROM PSALMS 22; 110; 118

WORDS OF ASSURANCE

⊰⊱⊷⊶⊷⊶⊱⊰

I will both lay me down in peace,
and sleep: for thou, Lord,
only makest me dwell in safety.

⊷⊶⊱

The Lord is my strength and my shield;
my heart trusted in him, and I am helped:
therefore my heart greatly rejoiceth;
and with my song will I praise him.

⊷⊶⊱

Behold, God is mine helper:
the Lord is with them that uphold my soul.

FROM PSALMS 4; 28; 54

PART IV

WORSHIP IN THE PSALMS

WHO WILL ASCEND
INTO THE HILL OF THE LORD?

⟨⟩

The earth is the Lord's,
and the fulness thereof; the world,
and they that dwell therein.
For he hath founded it upon the seas,
and established it upon the floods.

⟨⟩

Who shall ascend
into the hill of the Lord?
or who shall stand in his holy place?
He that hath clean hands,
and a pure heart;
who hath not lifted up his soul
unto vanity, nor sworn deceitfully.

He shall receive the blessing
from the Lord,
and righteousness from
the God of his salvation.
This is the generation
of them that seek him,
that seek thy face, O Jacob.

FROM PSALM 24

MY SOUL LONGETH
FOR THE COURTS OF THE LORD

How amiable are thy tabernacles,
O Lord of hosts! My soul longeth,
yea, even fainteth for the courts of the Lord:
my heart and my flesh
crieth out for the living God.

—•—

Yea, the sparrow hath found an house,
and the swallow a nest for herself,
where she may lay her young,
even thine altars, O Lord of hosts,
my King, and my God.
Blessed are they that dwell in thy house:
they will be still praising thee.

Blessed is the man
whose strength is in thee;
in whose heart are the ways of them.
Who passing through the valley of Baca
make it a well; the rain also filleth the pools.
They go from strength to strength,
every one of them in Zion
appeareth before God.

FROM PSALM 84

WORSHIP WITH A WARNING

O come, let us sing unto the Lord:
let us make a joyful noise
to the rock of our salvation.
Let us come before his presence
with thanksgiving,
and make a joyful noise
unto him with psalms.

For the Lord is a great God,
and a great King above all gods.
In his hand are the deep places
of the earth:
the strength of the hills is his also.
The sea is his, and he made it:
and his hands formed the dry land.

O come, let us worship
and bow down:
let us kneel before the Lord our maker.
For he is our God;
and we are the people of his pasture,
and the sheep of his hand.

⋅•⋅

Today if ye will hear his voice,
Harden not your heart,
as in the provocation,
and as in the day of temptation
in the wilderness . . ..

FROM PSALM 95

O SING UNTO THE LORD

~>===⊙===<~

O sing unto the Lord a new song:
sing unto the Lord, all the earth.
Sing unto the Lord, bless his name;
shew forth his salvation from day to day.
Declare his glory among the heathen,
his wonders among all people.

·~•~·

For the Lord is great,
and greatly to be praised:
he is to be feared above all gods.
For all the gods of the nations are idols:
but the Lord made the heavens.
Honour and majesty are before him:
strength and beauty are in his sanctuary.

Let the heavens rejoice,
and let the earth be glad;
let the sea roar, and the fulness thereof.
Let the field be joyful, and all that is therein:
then shall all the trees of the wood rejoice
Before the Lord: for he cometh,
for he cometh to judge the earth:
he shall judge the world with righteousness,
and the people with his truth.

FROM PSALM 96

I LOVE THE LORD

⊶⊷

I love the Lord,
because he hath heard my voice
and my supplications.
Because he hath inclined
his ear unto me,
therefore will I call upon him
as long as I live.

⋅◈⋅

The sorrows of death compassed me,
and the pains of hell gat hold upon me:
I found trouble and sorrow.
Then called I upon the
name of the Lord;
O Lord, I beseech thee, deliver my soul.

Gracious is the Lord,
and righteous;
yea, our God is merciful.
The Lord preserveth the simple:
I was brought low, and he helped me.

·•·

Return unto thy rest, O my soul;
for the Lord hath dealt
bountifully with thee.

·•·

Precious in the sight of the Lord
is the death of his saints.

FROM PSALM 116

A SONG OF THE REDEEMED

❧─═◉═─❧

O give thanks unto the Lord;
for he is good: because
his mercy endureth for ever.

∙❖∙

It is better to trust in the Lord
than to put confidence in man.
It is better to trust in the Lord
than to put confidence in princes.

∙❖∙

Thou hast thrust sore at me
that I might fall: but the Lord helped me.
The Lord is my strength and song,
and is become my salvation.

∙❖∙

Open to me the gates of righteousness:
I will go into them,
and I will praise the Lord:
This gate of the Lord,
into which the righteous shall enter.
I will praise thee:
for thou hast heard me,
and art become my salvation.

FROM PSALM 118

HEAR MY PRAYER, O LORD

⤝⊶⊙⊷⤞

*H*ear my prayer, O Lord,
give ear to my supplications;
in thy faithfulness answer me,
and in thy righteousness.
And enter not into judgment
with thy servant: for in thy sight
shall no man living be justified.

⋯•⋯

Hear me speedily, O Lord:
my spirit faileth:
hide not thy face from me,
lest I be like unto them
that go down into the pit.

Cause me to hear thy
lovingkindness in the morning;
for in thee do I trust:
cause me to know the way
wherein I should walk;
for I lift up my soul unto thee.

⋅•⋅

Deliver me, O Lord,
from mine enemies:
I flee unto thee to hide me.
Teach me to do thy will;
for thou art my God: thy spirit is good;
lead me into the land of uprightness.

FROM PSALM 143

PRAISE THE LORD!

*Praise ye the Lord.
Praise the Lord, O my soul.
While I live will I praise the Lord:
I will sing praises unto my God
while I have any being.

Put not your trust in princes,
nor in the son of man,
in whom there is no help.
His breath goeth forth,
he returneth to his earth;
in that very day his thoughts perish.

Happy is he that hath the God
of Jacob for his help,
whose hope is in the Lord his God:
Which made heaven, and earth,
the sea, and all that therein is:
which keepeth truth for ever:
Which executeth judgment for the oppressed:
which giveth food to the hungry.

•◆•

The Lord looseth the prisoners:
The Lord openeth the eyes of the blind:
the Lord raiseth them that are bowed down:
the Lord loveth the righteous.

FROM PSALM 146

INDEX OF PSALMS